WISE QUOTES: SOCRATES

(136 SOCRATES QUOTES)

Rowan Stevens

A multitude of books distracts the mind.

A system of morality which is based on relative emotional values is a mere illusion, a thoroughly vulgar conception which has nothing sound in it and nothing true.

All men's souls are immortal, but the souls of the righteous are immortal and divine.

All wars are fought for the acquisition of wealth.

An education obtained with money is worse than no education at all.

An honest man is always a child.

Are you not ashamed of heaping up the greatest amount of money and honor and reputation, and caring so little about wisdom and truth and the greatest improvement of the soul?

As to marriage or celibacy, let a man take which course he will, he will be sure to repent.

Bad men live that they may eat and drink, whereas good men eat and drink that they may live.

Be as you wish to seem.

Be kind, for everyone you meet is fighting a hard battle.

Be nicer than necessary to everyone you meet. Everyone is fighting some kind of battle.

Be slow to fall into friendship; but when thou art in, continue firm and constant.

Be the kind of person that you want people to think you are.

Beauty is a short-lived tyranny.

Beware the barrenness of a busy life.

By all means marry. If you get a good wife you will become happy, and if you get a bad one you will become a philosopher.

Call no man unhappy until he is married.

Children nowadays are tyrants. They contradict their parents, gobble their food, and tyrannize their teachers.

Contentment is natural wealth, luxury is artificial poverty.

Crito, I owe a cock to Asclepius; will you remember to pay the debt?

Death may be the greatest of all human blessings.

Do not do to others what angers you if done to you by others.

Education is the kindling of a flame, not the filling of a vessel.

Employ your time in improving yourself by other men's writings so that you shall come easily by what others have labored hard for.

Enjoy yourself — it's later than you think.

Envy is the ulcer of the soul.

Every action has its pleasures and its price.

Falling down is not a failure. Failure comes when you stay where you have fallen.

False words are not only evil in themselves, but they infect the soul with evil.

Fame is the perfume of heroic deeds.

From the deepest desires often come the deadliest hate.

Get not your friends by bare compliments, but by giving them sensible tokens of your love.

Give me beauty in the inward soul; may the outward and the inward man be at one.

Happiness is unrepentant pleasure.

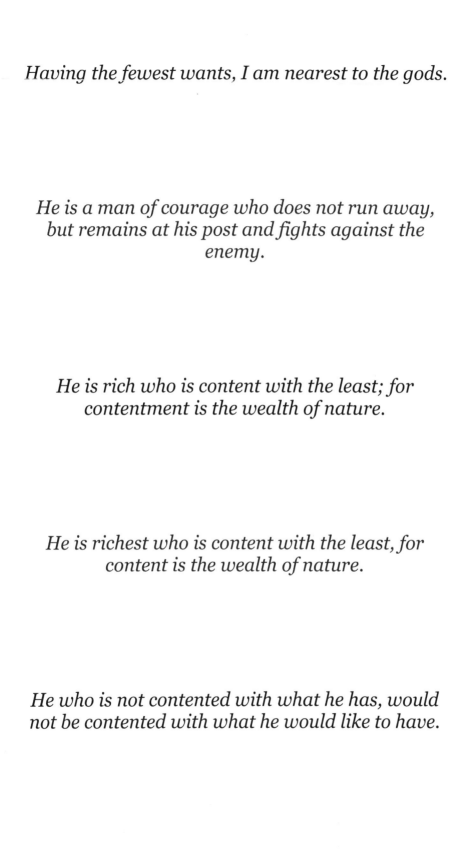

Having the fewest wants, I am nearest to the gods.

He is a man of courage who does not run away, but remains at his post and fights against the enemy.

He is rich who is content with the least; for contentment is the wealth of nature.

He is richest who is content with the least, for content is the wealth of nature.

He who is not contented with what he has, would not be contented with what he would like to have.

How many are the things I can do without!

I am not an Athenian, nor a Greek, but a citizen of the world.

I cannot teach anybody anything. I can only make them think.

I decided that it was not wisdom that enabled poets to write their poetry, but a kind of instinct or inspiration, such as you find in seers and prophets who deliver all their sublime messages without knowing in the least what they mean.

I know nothing except the fact of my ignorance.

I know that I am intelligent, because I know that I know nothing.

I only wish that ordinary people had an unlimited capacity for doing harm; then they might have an unlimited power for doing good.

I pray Thee, O God, that I may be beautiful within.

I was afraid that by observing objects with my eyes and trying to comprehend them with each of my other senses I might blind my soul altogether.

I was really too honest a man to be a politician and live.

If a man is proud of his wealth, he should not be praised until it is known how he employs it.

If all misfortunes were laid in one common heap whence everyone must take an equal portion, most people would be contented to take their own and depart.

If all our misfortunes were laid in one common heap whence everyone must take an equal portion, most people would be content to take their own and depart.

If I tell you that I would be disobeying the god and on that account it is impossible for me to keep quiet, you won't be persuaded by me, taking it that I am ionizing. And if I tell you that it is the greatest good for a human being to have discussions every day about virtue and the other things you hear me talking about, examining myself and others, and that the unexamined life is not livable for a human being, you will be even less persuaded.

If you don't get what you want, you suffer; if you get what you don't want, you suffer; even when you get exactly what you want, you still suffer because you can't hold on to it forever. Your mind is your predicament. It wants to be free of change. Free of pain, free of the obligations of life and death. But change is law and no amount of pretending will alter that reality.

If you want to be a good saddler, saddle the worst horse; for if you can tame one, you can tame all.

In childhood be modest, in youth temperate, in adulthood just, and in old age prudent.

is in knowing you know nothing.

It is not living that matters, but living rightly.

Know thyself.

Let him that would move the world first move himself.

Let him that would move the world, first move himself.

Life contains but two tragedies. One is not to get your heart's desire; the other is to get it.

Nature has given us two ears, two eyes, and but one tongue-to the end that we should hear and see more than we speak.

No evil can happen to a good man, either in life or after death. He and his are not neglected by the gods.

No man has the right to be an amateur in the matter of physical training. It is a shame for a man to grow old without seeing the beauty and strength of which his body is capable.

*No man undertakes a trade he has not learned,
even the meanest; yet everyone thinks himself
sufficiently qualified for the hardest of all trades,
that of government.*

Not life, but good life, is to be chiefly valued.

Nothing is to be preferred before justice.

*Once made equal to man, woman becomes his
superior.*

*One should never do wrong in return, nor mistreat
any man, no matter how one has been mistreated
by him.*

One thing only I know, and that is that I know nothing.

One who is injured ought not to return the injury, for on no account can it be right to do an injustice; and it is not right to return an injury, or to do evil to any man, however much we have suffered from him.

Ordinary people seem not to realize that those who really apply themselves in the right way to philosophy are directly and of their own accord preparing themselves for dying and death.

Ordinary people seem not to realize that those who really apply themselves in the right way to philosophy are directly and of their own accord preparing themselves for dying and death.

Our prayers should be for blessings in general, for God knows best what is good for us.

Prefer knowledge to wealth, for the one is transitory, the other perpetual.

Remember that there is nothing stable in human affairs; therefore avoid undue elation in prosperity, or undue depression in adversity.

Remember what is unbecoming to do is also unbecoming to speak of.

Remember, no human condition is ever permanent. Then you will not be overjoyed in good fortune nor too scornful in misfortune.

See one promontory, one mountain, one sea, one river and see all.

Silence is a profound melody, for those who can hear it above all the noise.

Slanderers do not hurt me because they do not hit me.

Smart people learn from everything and everyone, average people from their experiences, stupid people already have all the answers.

Sometimes you put walls up not to keep people out, but to see who cares enough to break them down.

Strong minds discuss ideas, average minds discuss events, weak minds discuss people.

The beginning of wisdom is a definition of terms.

The children now love luxury. They have bad manners, contempt for authority; they show disrespect for elders and love chatter in place of exercise.

The comic and the tragic lie inseparably close, like light and shadow.

The easiest and noblest way is not to be crushing others, but to be improving yourselves.

The end of life is to be like God, and the soul following God will be like Him.

The envious person grows lean with the fatness of their neighbor.

The fewer our wants the more we resemble the Gods.

The greatest blessing granted to mankind come by way of madness, which is a divine gift.

The greatest way to live with honor in this world is to be what we pretend to be.

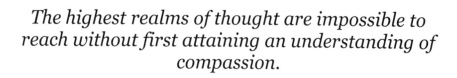

The highest realms of thought are impossible to reach without first attaining an understanding of compassion.

The hottest love has the coldest end.

The hour of departure has arrived and we go our ways; I to die, and you to live. Which is better? Only God knows.

The nearest way to glory is to strive to be what you wish to be thought to be.

The only good is knowledge and the only evil is ignorance.

The only true wisdom

The poets are only the interpreters of the gods.

*The secret of change is to focus all of your energy,
not on fighting the old, but on building the new.*

*The secret of happiness, you see, is not found in
seeking more, but in developing the capacity to
enjoy less.*

*The shortest and surest way to live with honor in
the world, is to be in reality what we would appear
to be; and if we observe, we shall find, that all
human virtues increase and strengthen themselves
by the practice of them.*

The unexamined life is not worth living.

*The way to gain a good reputation is to endeavor
to be what you desire to appear.*

*The years wrinkle our skin, but lack of enthusiasm
wrinkles our soul.*

*There are two kinds of disease of the soul, vice and
ignorance.*

*There is no possession more valuable than a good
and faithful friend.*

There is only one good, knowledge, and one evil, ignorance.

They are not only idle who do nothing, but they are idle also who might be better employed.

Think not those faithful who praise all thy words and actions, but those who kindly reprove thy faults.

Thou shouldst eat to live; not live to eat.

Through your rags I see your vanity.

To fear death, my friends, is only to think ourselves wise, without being wise: for it is to think that we know what we do not know. For anything that men can tell, death may be the greatest good that can happen to them: but they fear it as if they knew quite well that it was the greatest of evils. And what is this but that shameful ignorance of thinking that we know what we do not know?

To find yourself, think for yourself.

To move the world, we must move ourselves.

True wisdom comes to each of us when we realize how little we understand about life, ourselves, and the world around us.

True wisdom comes to each of us when we realize how little we understand about life, ourselves, and the world around us.

Understanding a question is half the answer.

Wars and revolutions and battles are due simply and solely to the body and its desires. All wars are undertaken for the acquisition of wealth; and the reason why we have to acquire wealth is the body, because we are slaves in its service.

We are in fact convinced that if we are ever to have pure knowledge of anything, we must get rid of the body and contemplate things by themselves with the soul by itself. It seems, to judge from the argument, that the wisdom which we desire and upon which we profess to have set our hearts will be attainable only when we are dead and not in our lifetime.

We can easily forgive a child who is afraid of the dark; the real tragedy of life is when men are afraid of the light.

We cannot live better than in seeking to become better.

Well I am certainly wiser than this man. It is only too likely that neither of us has any knowledge to boast of; but he thinks that he knows something which he does not know, whereas I am quite conscious of my ignorance. At any rate it seems that I am wiser than he is to this small extent, that I do not think that I know what I do not know.

What a lot of things there are a man can do without.

When desire, having rejected reason and overpowered judgement which leads to right, is set in the direction of the pleasure which beauty can inspire, and when again under the influence of its kindred desires it is moved with violent motion towards the beauty of corporeal forms, it acquires a surname from this very violent motion, and is called love.

When the debate is lost, slander becomes the tool of the loser.

When you want wisdom and insight as badly as you want to breathe, it is then you shall have it.

Whenever, therefore, people are deceived and form opinions wide of the truth, it is clear that the error has slid into their minds through the medium of certain resemblances to that truth.

Where there is reverence there is fear, but there is not reverence everywhere that there is fear, because fear presumably has a wider extension than reverence.

Whom do I call educated? First, those who manage well the circumstances they encounter day by day. Next, those who are decent and honorable in their intercourse with all men, bearing easily and good naturedly what is offensive in others and being as agreeable and reasonable to their associates as is humanly possible to be... those who hold their pleasures always under control and are not ultimately overcome by their misfortunes... those who are not spoiled by their successes, who do not desert their true selves but hold their ground steadfastly as wise and sober-minded men.

Wisdom begins in wonder.

Wonder is the beginning of wisdom.

Worthless people love only to eat and drink; people of worth eat and drink only to live.

Printed in Great Britain
by Amazon

71751735R00019